# Daily Pilgrimage

# to Purgatory

# Daily Pilgrimage
# to Purgatory

A Powerful Devotion for the Holy Souls

Nihil Obstat:

MA. SCHUMACHER, Censor Librorum

August 15, 1933

Imprimatur:

EDWARD F. HOBAN, Bishop of Rockford

Typography is the property of Seven Swords Publications, and may not be reproduced, in whole or in part, without written permission from the publisher.

seven swords publications
**www.susanpeekauthor.com**

*This reprint is lovingly dedicated to
the memory of William Millovitsch.
Please say a prayer for the repose of his soul.*

*May his soul,
and the souls of all the faithful departed,
through the mercy of God, rest in peace.
Amen.*

*"Oh! If all of us but knew how great is the power of the good souls in purgatory with the heart of God, and if we knew all the graces we can obtain through their intercession, they would not be so much forgotten! We must pray much for them, so that they may pray much for us."*

- St. John Vianney

# Origin of the Daily Pilgrimage to Purgatory

## Purpose

The purpose of this Daily Pilgrimage to Purgatory is to obtain relief and deliverance from Purgatory for the Holy Souls. Its secondary aim is to attain personal holiness, convert sinners, and acquire necessary spiritual and temporal graces.

## Background

In the writings of Saint Margaret Mary, we find the following exhortation:

*"In union with the divine Heart of Jesus make a short pilgrimage to Purgatory at night. Offer Him all your activities of the day and ask Him to apply His merits to the suffering souls. At the same time, implore them to obtain for you the grace to live and die in the love and friendship of this divine Heart. May He never find in you any resistance to His holy will, or any wish to thwart His designs in your regard. Fortunate*

*will you be, if you succeed in obtaining deliverance for some of these imprisoned souls, for you will gain as many friends in heaven."*

This pious practice, which Saint Margaret Mary recommended to her novices for the octave of All Souls, was introduced to the members of the Archconfraternity of Our Lady of the Sacred Heart in the year 1885. Since then, many of the faithful have made this pilgrimage daily. This worldwide Archconfraternity, therefore, would seem to have been chosen by divine Providence to obtain comfort and deliverance for many souls in Purgatory.

In a letter of recommendation, given on January 5, 1884, his Eminence, Cardinal Monaco la Valette, Vicar General of His Holiness, sanctioned the propagation of the *Daily Pilgrimage to Purgatory*. On October 8 of the following year, his successor, Cardinal Parochi deigned not only to honor us with a letter of approbation, but also delivered a splendid sermon on this practice in the church of Our Lady of the Sacred Heart in Rome, in which it had been introduced. May it please the divine Heart of Jesus to use this booklet as a means of spreading this work of sympathetic love for all the Holy Souls. May this most benevolent of hearts extend the fullness of His graces and blessings to all who, in any way, assist in its circulation.

A Daily Pilgrimage deserves to be propagated. My Christian friends who read these lines, priests, religious, or devout lay people, help to spread this devotion. It is so simple, and requires so little effort. You will be rewarded for it. Let at least one tiny drop of water trickle into Purgatory every day. If everyone does this, many souls will be released, and a refreshing stream of grace will flow without ceasing through that prison of fire.

# Advantages of a Daily Pilgrimage

## A Daily Pilgrimage to Purgatory is:

### Short

Requires little more of your time than an ordinary prayer, a religious thought, or a devout ejaculation.

### Easy

Can be practiced by anyone without effort, regardless of age or state of life, at any time, and in any place.

### Comforting

Requires no more than: 1) to descend in spirit for a few moments into Purgatory, 2) to petition God to send light, relief and peace to the holy souls to relieve them of their sufferings, and 3) to hasten the hour of their deliverance.

### Holy

Is in accordance with the wishes of the Sacred Heart and increases His honor. He is our companion on this pilgrimage. We share in his love and receive from Him light, relief, and peace for the suffering souls.

## Generous

Offers to the Sacred Heart every meritorious deed performed in the course of our day. This places our prayers, mortifications, good works, alms, and suffrages of every kind at His disposal on behalf of the Holy Souls.

## Inexhaustible

Implores Our Lord and Savior to apply to the Holy Souls the infinite merits of His Life, His Passion, and His Death. It also implores the Blessed Virgin Mary, Saint Joseph, and all The Saints to apply the merits of their lives and suffering.

## Efficient

Relieves the sufferings of these holy souls so well, that they long for this new "remedy." This is what Saint Margaret Mary calls devotion to the Sacred Heart.

## Meritorious

Increases our own merits in the same measure as the pious thoughts it inspires, the good disposition it creates, and the acts of virtue it prompts.

## Constant

Occurs during every moment of the day and night. Somewhere on earth members of the Archconfraternity of Our Lady of the Sacred Heart pray for our departed friends according to our intention via an uninterrupted sequence of holy Masses, Stations of the Cross, good works, prayers and indulgences. Those whose death we mourn will never be forgotten.

## Church Approved

Approved by many bishops. His Eminence, the Cardinal Vicar of his Holiness, has recommended it twice in a most explicit manner. The Holy Father himself has deigned to bestow the richest privileges upon the altar of the Holy Souls in the Church of Our Lady of the Sacred Heart in Rome.

## Favored by God

Numerous spiritual and temporal favors have manifested, again and again, how pleasing this practice is to the Sacred Heart. One may use it with confidence as a means of obtaining the conversion of a sinner, the restoration of health, or a special grace. Very effective also is the promise to promote this devotion if a petition is heard. If the Lord rewards in this life the gift or a cup of cold water, given in His name to the poor, He certainly will reward, even more generously, the help offered for His sake to the Holy Souls.

## Salutary

Ensures the perpetual gratitude of the Holy Souls, who will pray for us, especially after their entrance into eternal happiness; in particular will they endeavor to obtain for us the grace of a happy death.

# Preparing for your Daily Pilgrimage to Purgatory

(Any of the following acts or a similar act will suffice.)

## Prayer

*O Saint Margaret Mary, whom the Lord has chosen to reveal to the whole world all the treasures hidden in his merciful heart of Love! O thou who hast heard how the Holy Souls in Purgatory begged for this new remedy, the devotion to the Sacred Heart which relieves them so effectively of their torments! O thou who hast set free so many of these poor prisoners by practicing this devotion: obtain for us the grace to make this Pilgrimage worthily in the company of the Sacred Heart of Jesus. Amen.*

Unite your own intentions with those of the faithful who make this pilgrimage daily.

## Consecration of the Day

*Divine Heart of Jesus, in making this pilgrimage with Thee as my Companion, I consecrate to Thee all my thoughts, words and actions of the entire day. I pray Thee to unite my small merits with Thine and to apply them to the Holy Souls, especially the soul of Thy servant, N. Likewise, do I entreat you, holy souls, to help me obtain the grace to persevere in love and loyalty toward the Sacred Heart, by submitting readily and without complaint to whatever designs He may have in my regard.*

## Offering

*Eternal Father, we offer Thee the Blood, Passion and Death of Jesus Christ and the sorrows of the most holy Mary and Saint Joseph in payment for our sins, in suffrage for the holy souls in Purgatory, for the wants of our Holy Mother the Church and for the conversion of Sinners. Amen.*

## Ejaculations

*May the Sacred Heart of Jesus be loved everywhere.*

*Our Lady of the Sacred Heart, pray for us.*

*Saint Joseph, model and patron of those who love the Sacred Heart, pray for us.*

## Preparatory Meditation

Let us, for a moment, in company with the Sacred Heart, descend in spirit into the consuming flames of Purgatory. How many of these souls are beginning their painful imprisonment this very moment! I know many of them have been there for a long time and shall be there for a longer time to come! And what a holy legion almost entirely purified and cleansed at the present moment, shall rise to heaven this very day! How happy the Holy Souls are! They are friends of God and they have escaped hell forever. Eventually, they are certain to obtain eternal happiness. Yet, they are still miserable. They must still suffer temporal punishment for sins that have been already forgiven. The gates of their heavenly fatherland are still closed to them; they aresentenced to expiating fire. Behold them in their present plight! Listen to their lamentations! Speak a word of friendship and sympathy to them and hasten to their assistance!

Daily visits to Purgatory

for each day of the week

# Sunday

***Holy Souls in Purgatory, is there anything you regret when you think of your life on earth?***

"I deeply regret wasted time. I did not consider it so precious, so fleeting, or so irretrievable. Wasted time made my life worth only half of what is might have been. Oh, I wish I had only realized it then! If only I could return to earth, how differently I would use the time given me! Oh, Precious, Time! Today I know how to appreciate you. You were purchased with the blood of Christ! You were given to me for the sole purpose of loving God, sanctifying myself, and edifying my neighbor. Alas, I abused you by sinning. I craved vanity, pleasures, and trifles. I dreamed dreams that now cause me bitter reproaches and remorse. Precious, Time Wasted, Time How heavily you weigh upon me now! How it grieves me to have lost you through my own fault! Fleeting time passes so quickly on earth, but drags so slowly in this place of excruciating torments ! Formerly, years seemed like days to me. My whole life vanished like a dream.

Hours now seem like years, and days like centuries. I must now suffer, weep, and wait, until I redeem the last minute of wasted time. Oh, how long shall my exile last! Oh, irretrievable, Time! I relied on my last years on earth to do penance; but the thread of my life was severed at a moment when I expected it least! Oh, precious, Time! You were given to me to acquire treasures and graces without number, but now you are lost for me forever."

"You, who still live on earth, do not waste the gift of time, which has cost Jesus such a high price, and for which you too will have to suffer in Purgatory if you imitate our carelessness. You, who are privileged to live during a time which is pre-eminently devoted to the Sacred Heart, during these last centuries when He has revealed to the world His love in its fullness: intercede for us that we may obtain the merits of at least one of these days, in which His grace is so freely and abundantly offered you."

# Pious Exercises

## Resolution:

Today I will do everything possible to assist the souls of priests, religious and all those in Purgatory who have been faithful to this devotion all their lives. I also recommend myself to those who are entering heaven at this moment.

## Thought for the Day:

The sufferings of the souls in Purgatory are so great that a single day appears to them like a thousand years.

## Exercise:

Use a few moments of your time to make ejaculations in honor of the divine Heart for the comfort and consolation of the Holy Souls.

## Special Intention:

Implore the divine Heart of Jesus to grant relief to the most forsaken soul in Purgatory.

## Motive:

The greater the abandonment of a soul, the greater

will be its gratitude towards you. That soul will obtain for you the privilege that God will never abandon you through withdrawal of His grace, and you will never abandon God by committing sin.

## Prayers:

*(Any Prayers for the Holy Souls May be Used)*

*Oh Lord God Almighty, I pray Thee, by the Precious Blood that Thy divine Son Jesus shed in the garden, deliver the souls in Purgatory and especially that soul which is most destitute of spiritual aid; and vouchsafe to bring it to Thy glory, there to praise and bless Thee forever. Amen. Our Father, Hail Mary . .*

De Profundis Psalm 129:

Out of the depths I have cried unto Thee, O Lord. Lord hear my voice. Let Thine ears be attentive to the voice of my supplication. If Thou, O Lord, shall mark our iniquities, O Lord, who can abide it? For with Thee there is mercy; and by reason of Thy law, I have waited on Thee, O Lord. My soul hath waited on His word; my soul hath hoped in the Lord. From the morning watch even unto night, let Israel hope in the Lord. For with the Lord there is mercy; and with Him is plentiful redemption. And he shall redeem Israel from all his iniquities.

V. Eternal rest grant unto them, O Lord.

R. And let perpetual light shine upon them.

**Ejaculation:**

Sweet Heart of Jesus, make me love Thee ever more and more.

# Monday

***Holy Souls in Purgatory, is there anything you regret when you think of your life on earth?***

"I deeply regret my extravagance in the use of earthly possessions. My fortune, my health, my talent, my position in the world, the influence I had, my relatives, my servants, in a word, everything could have been of spiritual benefit to me if only I had known how to use it for the greater honor of the Divine Heart. How many graces could I have drawn upon myself! This I neglected to do, and at the hour of my death, all my possessions have come to naught. Oh, were I but rich today in these my former possession! Would that I could use them to hasten even for one moment, the hour of my deliverance; to increase, even by one degree, the glory which God has in store for me; to awaken if only in one soul now living in the world, the devotion to the divine Heart of Jesus."

"My friends, your fortunes are still at your disposal. Use them for the support of your neighbor by generously giving alms to the poor. Use them for the greater honor of God as pious offerings designated for the propagation of the devotion to His Sacred Heart throughout the world."

## Pious Exercises

### Resolution:

Today I will do everything possible to assist the souls of the faithful departed from all parts of Europe. I also recommend myself to those who are entering heaven at this moment.

### Thought for the day:

*"The gates of heaven are opened by alms."*

- St. John Chrysostom

### Exercise:

Give alms for the propagation of the devotion to the divine Heart of Jesus.

### Special Intention:

Pray for the soul that is nearest to heaven.

### Motive:

The closer a soul is to the end of its sufferings, the more ardently it will long for union with the Sacred Heart. Remove, therefore, by your prayers, the obstacles still in its way. In return, it will obtain for you the grace to sever the ties that now prevent you from giving yourself entirely to God.

### Prayer:

*O Lord God Almighty, I pray Thee, by the Precious Blood which Thy divine Son Jesus shed in His cruel scourging, deliver the souls in Purgatory, and that soul especially which is nearest to its entrance into Thy glory; that so it may forthwith begin to praise and bless Thee forever. Amen. Our Father, Hail Mary . . .*

### Ejaculation:

Sweet Heart of Mary, be my salvation!

# Tuesday

***Holy Souls in Purgatory, is there anything you regret when you think of your life on earth?***

"I deeply regret my neglect of so many splendid graces. I was offered graces in such abundance at every moment of my life and with such loving admonitions: spiritual regeneration, vocation and sacraments; word of God, holy inspirations and good examples; graces to protect me in danger, to help me in temptations; the grace of forgiveness for my sins, and indulgences so easily gained. What an incalculable number of the most incredible graces! Some of them I refused. Others I accepted with coldness. Unfortunately, I misused most of them. I preferred earthly possessions to the eternal. How I deceived myself! Oh, could I but for one moment quench my thirst at the fountains of mercy flowing from the Sacred Heart! Unfortunately, sinner, spurn those fountains as I spurned them."

"You, who behold the inexhaustible stream of graces flow by, why do you not draw from it a few drops for yourself!"

Consider what Saint Margaret Mary says: "It is certain that everyone on earth could obtain salutary graces without number, if he but had a grateful love for Jesus Christ, such as is manifested by those who love and venerate His Sacred Heart."

## Pious Exercises

### Resolution:

Today I will do everything possible to assist the souls of the faithful departed from all parts of Asia, particularly from Palestine and from countries infested with idolatry, schism and heresy. I also recommend myself to those who are entering heaven at this moment.

### Thought for the day:

*"The benefit of a single grace is greater than all the material value of the whole world."*

- Saint Thomas Aquinas

**Exercise:**

To relieve the Holy Souls of their sufferings, I shall offer them today, by way of suffrage, the benefit of some indulgence gained by prayers or some devotional exercise in honor of the divine Heart of Jesus.

**Special Intention:**

Pray for the soul in Purgatory that is farthest from eternal rest.

**Motive:**

Let yourself be moved by the abandonment, resignation and humility with which that soul bears

its long suffering: it will be grateful to you. Happy will you be, if it obtains for you the virtue of humility in this world, so that you may be exalted in the next.

**Prayer:**

*O Lord Almighty, I pray Thee, by the Precious Blood shed by Thy divine Son Jesus in the bitter crowning of thorns, please deliver the souls in Purgatory. Please especially deliver that soul that would be the last to depart out of that place of suffering, so it might not tarry too long before it comes to praise Thee in thy glory and bless Thee forever. Amen.*

*Eternal Father, I offer Thee the Precious Blood of Jesus Christ in satisfaction for my sins, in supplication for the Holy Souls in Purgatory, and for the needs of the Holy Church. Our Father, Hail Mary . . .*

## Ejaculation:

Eternal Father, I offer Thee the Precious Blood of Jesus Christ in satisfaction for my sins, in supplication for the Holy Souls in Purgatory, and for the needs of the Holy Church.

# Wednesday

***Holy Souls in Purgatory, is there anything you regret when you think of your life on earth?***

"I deeply regret the evil that I committed. In the world, evil seemed so easy, so pleasant. In the midst of pleasures, I silenced the voice of conscience. Today my faults weigh me down; their bitterness torments me; their memory persecutes and tortures me. Mortal sins, forgiven, but not atoned for, venial sins, and small imperfections. It is too late to detest you in Purgatory! Just punishment must now take its course. Oh, if I could return to life again! No promise, be it ever so tempting, no riches, no flattery could induce me to commit even the smallest sin!"

"My friends, you who are still free to choose between God and the world, gaze upon the crown of thorns, upon the cross, and upon all the sufferings your sins have brought upon the Sacred Heart! Think of the sorrow these sins and faults will cause you in Purgatory and you will be able to avoid them without effort."

If you long for the grace to resist Satan when he tempts you, consider what Saint Margaret Mary says. "I cannot believe that persons consecrated to this divine Heart will ever be lost; neither do I believe that they will fall into the hands of Satan by committing a mortal sin, after having given themselves entirely to Him. For they will make every effort to honor, love, and glorify this divine Heart and to follow his designs in their regard willingly and without reserve."

## Pious Exercises

### Resolution:

Today I will do everything possible to assist the souls of the faithful departed from Africa, particularly from those countries in Africa that were formerly Catholic, and are now returning to our holy Faith. I also recommend myself to those who are entering heaven at this moment.

### Thought for the day:

*"What doth it profit a man, if he gains the whole*

*world and suffers the loss of his own soul?"* (Math. 16: 25.)

### Exercise:

Make an act of contrition in union with the souls in Purgatory and before the Sacred Heart.

### Special intention:

Pray for the soul richest in merits.

### Motive:

The more exalted a soul is in heaven, the more effective will be its request for true love of God for you, without which there is no real merit.

### Prayer:

*O Lord God Almighty, I pray Thee, by the Precious Blood shed by Thy divine Son Jesus in the streets of Jerusalem, when He carried the Cross upon His sacred shoulders, please deliver the souls in Purgatory. Please especially deliver that soul that is richest in merits before Thee, so in that throne of glory that awaits it, it may magnify Thee and bless Thee forever. Amen. Our Father, Hail Mary . . .*

**Ejaculation:**

Jesus, Mary, and Joseph. I give you my heart and my soul. Jesus, Mary, and Joseph, assist me in my last agony. Jesus, Mary, and Joseph, may I breathe forth my soul in peace with you.

# Thursday

***Holy Souls in Purgatory, is there anything you regret when you think of your life on earth?***

"I deeply regret the scandal that I gave! Oh, if I had to grieve over my own faults only ... If only I would have prevented, in the hour of my health, the disastrous consequences of the scandal of which I was the cause. If only I could detain from this place of darkness the many souls that followed my sad example and listened to my pernicious teachings! But, no! Through my fault, the evil goes on, and perhaps, will spread over a period of years and centuries. Now, I have to give an account of all the sins for which I am to blame! Oh, were I but able to let my sad words resound unto the ends of the earth and to wander through the world as a preacher of penance! With what untiring zeal would I labor among souls to estrange them from evil and return them to virtue."

"Oh, you my friends on earth, who come to visit me in this dark prison in order to let a ray of salutary light shine upon me, you shall find in the Sacred Heart the surest and easiest way of bringing God back to as many souls as I have led into sin by bad example! Tell them, "His divine Heart is a fortress and a sanctuary for those who desire to escape divine justice by seeking refuge in Him. For the number of sins committed at the present time is so great, they challenge a just Creator to punish the sinner swiftly and severely."

## Pious Exercises

### Resolution:

Today I will do everything possible to assist the souls of the faithful departed from North and South America, especially those from my native town. I also recommend myself to those who are entering heaven at this moment.

### Thought for the day:

*"The Son of man will render to everyone according to his works."* (Math. 16:27)

**Exercise:**

Give to someone a picture or a book treating of the Sacred Heart.

**Special Intention:**

Pray for the soul that had the greatest devotion to the Most Blessed Sacrament.

**Motive:**

That soul will obtain for you the grace to receive Holy Communion worthily at the hour of death as a pledge of your eternal salvation.

**Prayer:**

*O Lord God Almighty, I pray Thee, by the Precious Blood of Thy divine Son Jesus, which He gave with His own hands upon the eve of His Passion to His beloved Apostles to be their food and drink, and which He left to His whole Church to be a perpetual sacrifice and live-giving food of His own faithful people, deliver the souls in Purgatory. Please especially deliver that one soul that was most devoted to this mystery of infinite love, that it may with Thy same divine Son, and with Thy Holy Spirit, ever praise Thee for Thy love therein in eternal glory, Amen.*

*Our Father Hail Mary . . .*

**Ejaculation:**

My Jesus! Mercy!

# Friday

***Holy Souls in Purgatory, is there anything you regret when you think of your life on earth?***

"I deeply regret my neglect of acts of mortification. How easy they would have been on earth, but how difficult they are now in Purgatory. Here the smallest suffering is more poignant than the crudest torments on earth. In the world, it meant only patience and resignation in the hardships and adversities of my life. It meant only giving from my surplus to the poor, and devoting myself to works of atonement. It meant only gaining Indulgences and performing works of piety. Nothing could have been easier, and my Purgatory would have been shortened considerably. If God would but grant me the grace to exchange the years during which I must still remain in this place of sorrow for as many years of life on earth! No commands would be too severe for me; no pains could frighten me; the most difficult works of penance would be sweet and give me comfort at the thought of this consuming fire."

"You, who now smart under the insignificant trials and hardships of this life, you who now earn your daily bread by the sweat of your brow, rejoice! The smallest suffering endured in the spirit of atonement and offered to the Sacred Heart in the spirit of expiation will save you from a long and painful Purgatory!"

## Pious Exercises

### Resolution:

Today I will do everything possible to assist the souls of the faithful departed from the far distant countries of Oceania, particularly from the most difficult, severely tried Catholic mission districts. I also recommend myself to those who are entering heaven at this moment.

### Thought for the day:

*"Bring forth therefore worthy fruits of penance."* (Luke 3: 8.)

### Exercise:

Offer to the Sacred Heart a little act of mortification

for the relief of the suffering souls in Purgatory.

## Special Intention:

Pray for the souls for which you are most bound to pray.

## Motive:

If you are indebted to these souls by an obligation of justice, do not postpone it, because this may call down the wrath of God upon yourself.

## Prayer:

*O Lord God Almighty, I pray Thee, by the Precious Blood that Thy divine Son shed on this day upon the wood of the cross, especially from His most sacred hands and feet, deliver the souls in Purgatory. Please especially deliver that one soul for which I am most bound to pray; that no neglect of mine may hinder it from praising Thee in Thy glory and from blessing Thee forever. Amen. Our Father Hail, Mary . . .*

## Ejaculation:

Jesus, meek and humble of heart, make my heart like unto thine.

# Saturday

***Holy Souls in Purgatory, is there anything you regret when you think of your life on earth?***

"I deeply regret the little amount of charity I have shown towards the Holy Souls during my life on earth. I could have been of such great service to them, since a Catholic can bring so much light and peace to these poor, suffering prisoners. I could have helped them by my prayers, mortifications, alms, good works, holy communions, and holy Masses. I could have had Masses said for the Holy Souls or I could have attended Masses celebrated in honor of the Sacred Heart and offered them for the Holy Souls. I would have obtained numerous graces that would have made it easier for me to avoid sin. Moreover, I would have deserved a much shorter and less painful Purgatory, and now I would receive a much greater share in the prayers that are said for us wherever there are Catholics. Oh, could I but return to the world to help the Holy Souls! I certainly would interest myself in their sad plight! What devout prayers would

I say for them! How solicitous I would be to awaken in the faithful the tenderest sympathy and pity for them."

## Pious Exercises

### Resolution:

Today I will do everything possible to assist the souls of the faithful departed from the missions of the World. I also recommend myself to those who are entering heaven at this moment.

### Thought for the day:

The guilt-burdened brothers of innocent Joseph spoke to one another, "We deserve to suffer these things, because we have sinned against our brother, seeing the anguish of his soul, when he besought us, and we would not hear; therefore, this affliction has come upon us." (Gen. 42:21)

### Exercise:

Spread, as much as possible, this devotional booklet, *Daily Pilgrimage to Purgatory*. The Holy Souls will be grateful to you.

### Special Intention:

Pray for the soul that had the greatest devotion to Our Lady of the Sacred Heart.

### Motive:

In praying for that devoted soul, you cause the Mother of God great delight. She will obtain for you, through the intercession of that soul, the grace of a true devotion to the Sacred Heart.

### Prayer:

*O Lord God Almighty, I beseech Thee, by the Precious Blood that gushed forth from the side of Thy Divine Son Jesus, in the sight of, and to the extreme pain of His most Holy Mother, deliver the souls in Purgatory. Please, especially deliver the soul that was the most devout to Our Lady of the Sacred Heart and Queen of Heaven, that it may soon attain unto Thy glory, there to praise Thee in her, and her in Thee, world without end. Amen. Our Father, Hail Mary . . .*

### Ejaculation:

Our Lady of the Sacred Heart, pray for us!

# The Heroic Act of Charity in Favor of the Holy Souls in Purgatory

The Heroic Act of Charity is the most beautiful and most effective manifestation of devotion to the Holy Souls, as well as of love of God and neighbor in general. For you who have not made it yet, we give the following explanation.

## Purpose of the Heroic Act of Charity

The heroic act of charity on behalf of the souls in Purgatory consists of a voluntary offering, made by one of the faithful in their favor, of all works of satisfaction done in this life, as well as of all suffrages that will be offered after death. By this act, the faithful person deposits all these works and suffrages into the hands of the Blessed Virgin, so she can distribute them on behalf of those holy souls whom it is her good pleasure to deliver from the pains of Purgatory. At the same time, the faithful person declares that by this personal offering he or she forgoes on their behalf only the special and personal benefit of those works of satisfaction. Therefore, if he is a priest, he will not be hindered from applying the Holy Sacrifice of the Mass according to the intention of those who give him alms for that purpose. Every meritorious act performed in the state of sanctifying grace and with a good intention, gains for us the following spiritual privileges:

• An increase in sanctifying grace and heavenly glory.

• Many graces of body and soul for ourselves and for others.

• Remission of temporal punishment for our sins. (Only this third fruit, the satisfactory or expiatory part of the works that we accomplish is conceded or applied to the souls in Purgatory, whereas the fruit of merit and impetration (of prayer), remains ours. The heroic act therefore does not prevent us from praying for ourselves or for others, and it does not prevent others from sharing in our good works.)

# Remarks Regarding the Heroic Act of Charity

In making the heroic act and desiring to gain the indulgences attached to it, one foregoes in truth and in fact, without reservation of any kind, and without exception, the special and personal benefits of all works of satisfaction and suffrage, and deposits them as a voluntary offering to God in the hands of the Blessed Virgin.

This act of charity is not a vow and does not bind under sin. It may be revoked at any time. It stands to reason, however, that, by doing so, one can no longer gain the indulgences attached to the heroic act.

## Indulgences from the Heroic Act of Charity :

Priests who have made this offering may enjoy the benefits of the privileged altar personally every day of the year.

All the faithful who have made this act may gain:

1. A plenary indulgence applicable only to the departed, every day that they receive Holy Communion, provided they visit a church or public oratory and pray for the intention of the Sovereign Pontiff.

2. The faithful will gain a plenary indulgence every Monday, if they hear Mass in suffrage for the souls in Purgatory and fulfill the usual conditions. Sick people, old people, those living in the country, travelers, prisoners, and so forth, who cannot hear Mass on Monday may offer to this end that of Sunday.

3. All indulgences granted, or to be granted, and gained by the faithful who have made this offering, are applicable to the Holy Souls in Purgatory, even when this faculty is not stated in the formula or decree of the concession of such indulgences.

## Motives for Making the Heroic Act of Charity:

1. You gain many indulgences.

2. Innumerable souls are quickly released from Purgatory. Heaven is filled with new saints, who will glorify and praise God for all eternity, on your behalf.

3. You will gain the special love of the Holy Trinity, of Our Savior, and of all the saints and you have the promise of Our Lord applied to you. "Blessed are the merciful, for they shall obtain mercy." (Math. 5:7.)

4. After you have made the heroic act, the Holy Souls will become your debtors. In Heaven they will labor that you may not be lost, that you shall not suffer Purgatory at all, or at least that you be released from it soon.

5. The Blessed Virgin receives an increase of veneration, since she will be proclaimed, loved, and invoked as the most loving Queen of the Holy Souls and sweet dispenser of our merits to them. There can be no doubt that she will have a special affection for those who love and honor her in this way, both while they are in this world and after they have passed into eternity.

## Unnecessary Apprehension Regarding the Heroic Act of Charity :

Do not be afraid that you will suffer any loss by this act of charity. Neither need you fear that you yourself will be in danger of having to endure a long and painful Purgatory. On the contrary, you can only gain by it, since you will enjoy the special love of the Most Holy Trinity, of Our Savior, of the Blessed Virgin, and of all the saints. Who shall fare better in the end? He who relies solely on justice of God? ... or he who heroically offers his merits to the Holy Souls and trusts entirely in God's infinite mercy and generosity? The latter without a doubt. In making the heroic act of charity, therefore, you have nothing to fear for yourself; you can only gain by it. Nor need you fear that the souls of your relatives, friends, and benefactors will be slighted in the least.

The Blessed Virgin does not distribute arbitrarily the good works offered for the Holy Souls, but according to that measure of charity and justice that God himself employs in the distribution of His graces. She will therefore favor with your merits preferably those souls towards whom you have special obligations.

Many persons, distinguished by their position, learning, and holiness, have made this heroic act in favor of the Holy Souls and will not regret it in eternity. Follow their example, and likewise offer the atoning merits of your good works for the comfort and deliverance of the Holy Souls.

No special formula for making the heroic act is prescribed. For your convenience, however, we herewith give the formula taken from the works of Saint Alphonsus de Liguori. Its briefness lends itself to a frequent and profitable renewal of this act.

## The Heroic Act of Charity

Oh my God, in union with the merits of Jesus and Mary, I offer Thee for the souls in Purgatory, all my satisfactory works, as well as those which may be applied to me by others during my life, and after my death. And, so as to be more agreeable to the Divine Heart of Jesus and more helpful to the departed, I place them all in the hands of the merciful Virgin Mary.

## Invocations for the Holy Souls

We beseech Thee, O Lord, help the souls detained in the fire of Purgatory, whom Thou hast redeemed with Thy Precious Blood.

Dear Lord Jesus, grant them (or him) eternal rest.

# Appendix:

## Two devotions to help the Holy Souls and avoid Purgatory ourselves

# The Way of the Cross

*Many saints have assured us that one of the most efficacious ways to help the Holy Souls is to make the Stations of the Cross for them. This devotion not only has the power to release and alleviate many souls from Purgatory, but is immensely pleasing to Our Lord and salutary for us, as the following promises show:*

## Promises of Our Lord to those devoted to the Stations of the Cross

1. I will grant everything that is asked of Me with faith, when making The Way of the Cross.

2. I promise Eternal Life to those who pray from time to time, The Way of the Cross.

3. I will follow them everywhere in life and I will help them, especially at the hour of death.

4. Even if they have more sins than the blades of grass in the fields and the grains of sand in the sea, all of them will be erased by the Way of the Cross.

*(Note: Mortal sins must still be confessed and absolved.)*

5. Those who pray The Way of the Cross often will have a special glory in Heaven.

6. I will deliver them from Purgatory, indeed if they go there at all, the first Tuesday or Friday after their death.

7. I will bless them at each Way of the Cross, and My blessing will follow them everywhere on earth and, after their death, in Heaven for all Eternity.

8. At the hour of death I will not permit the devil to tempt them; I will lift all power from him in order that they will repose tranquilly in My Arms.

9. If they pray it with true love, I will make of each one of them a living Ciborium in which it will please Me to pour My grace.

10. I will fix My Eyes on those who pray The Way of the Cross often; My hands will always be open to protect them.

11. As I am nailed to the Cross, so also will I always be with those who honor Me in making The Way of the Cross frequently.

12. They will never be able to separate themselves from Me, for I will give them the grace never again to commit a Mortal sin.

13. At the hour of death I will console them with My Presence and we will go together to Heaven. Death will be sweet to all those who have honored Me during their lives by praying The Way of the Cross.

14. My soul will be a protective shield for them, and will always help them, whenever they have recourse.

*These promises were revealed by Our Lord to Brother Estanislao, a young and very holy Spanish Brother of the Christian Schools who, after offering himself as a victim soul, died in the odor of sanctity at age 24 in 1927. While the promises have not yet been officially approved by the Church, the faithful can nonetheless piously hope to receive these great privileges and graces, and can certainly be assured that devotion to Our Lord's sufferings on His way to Calvary will immensely profit themselves and the Holy Souls alike!*

# Devotion to the 7 Sorrows of Our Lady

According to St. Bridget of Sweden, the Blessed Virgin Mary has promised to grant seven graces to the souls who honor her daily by thinking of her seven sorrows and reciting a *Hail Mary* for each one. The last two promises (in bold print) are of special interest to souls hoping to obtain a happy death and avoid Purgatory.

## Here are Our Lady's Seven Sorrows:

1. The prophecy of Simeon that a sword shall pierce Mary's soul

2. The flight into Egypt to save the Infant Jesus from Herod

3. The loss of Jesus in the Temple for three days when He was twelve years old

4. Jesus carries His Cross to Calvary

5. The Crucifixion of Jesus

6. Jesus is taken down from the Cross and placed in Mary's arms

7. Jesus is laid in the tomb

# And here are Our Lady's Seven Promises:

I will grant peace to their families.

They will be enlightened about the Divine Mysteries.

I will console them in their pains and I will accompany them in their work.

I will give them as much as they ask for as long as it does not oppose the adorable will of my Divine Son or the sanctification of their souls.

I will defend them in their spiritual battles with the infernal enemy and I will protect them at every instant of their lives.

**I will visibly help them at the moment of their death.** They will see the face of their Mother.

I have obtained this grace from my divine Son, that **those who propagate this devotion to my tears and dolors, will be taken directly from this earthly life to eternal happiness** since all their sins will be forgiven and my Son and I will be their eternal consolation and joy.

## Other Ways to Help the Holy Souls

Spread the devotion to the Sacred Heart, so dear and beneficial to the suffering souls.

Distribute this booklet, *Daily Pilgrimage to Purgatory,* or other good books about Purgatory.

Ask your parish priest to offer the Holy Sacrifice of the Mass for the Holy Souls, or, if you're unable to do that, attend a Mass for them.

Offer your Holy Communion or Rosary for the Souls in Purgatory.

# Books About Purgatory

*Read Me or Rue It* by Fr. Paul O'Sullivan

*How to Avoid Purgatory* by Fr. Paul O'Sullivan

*Purgatory* by Fr. F.X. Schouppe

*Hungry Souls* by Gerard J.M. Van den Aardweg

**Books by Susan Tassone**

***Tortured Soul*** **by Theresa Linden (An excellent novel based on true apparitions from Purgatory)**

Made in United States
Orlando, FL
27 February 2023